Other-Wise

Other-Wise

Poems by

Robbi Nester

Kelsay Books

© 2017 Robbi Nester. All rights reserved. This material may not be reproduced in any form, published, reprinted, recorded, performed, broadcast, rewritten or redistributed without the explicit permission of Robbi Nester. All such actions are strictly prohibited by law.

Cover art: Untitled, 2010, by Ira Joel Haber

ISBN:13-978-1-945752-87-2

Kelsay Books
Aldrich Press
www.kelsaybooks.com

Acknowledgments

Journals:

Artemis: "Flyway"
Boston Literary Review: "8 Notes to Myself at Twenty"
Cadence Collective: "Sea Angel"
Danse Macabre: "How to Get There"
3 Elements Review: "Fistulated Cow," "The Wrong Job"
Houseboat: "Consolation," "Evolution," "Fire," "Mysteries"
Life and Legend: "Sounding," "Succulents"
The Light Ekphrastic: "The World to Come"
Poemeleon: "Note to Self," "Lemon"
Poetry Storehouse: "Another Statistic"
Prompt and Circumstance: "Leavings"
Silver Birch Press: "Medusa," "Driving Lesson"
Verse-Virtual: "Body Knowledge," "Invader," "July," "Making Do," "Repair," "Tradition"

Anthologies:

Attack of the Poems, edited by Raundi Moore Kondo: "Summer Camp"
Dads of Disability, edited by Gary Dietz: "Letter to My Son"
The Liberal Media Made Me Do It!: " "Unenforceable," "Humane"
Prompt and Circumstance: "Leavings," "Evolution," and "Feather and Flock"
Safe to Chew: "Spring-Fever"
Short Poems Ain't Got Nobody to Love: "Seal"
True: Truth Serum, Volume 1: "Books Cannot Save Us"

Honors and Awards:

"Leavings" received first prize in *Prompt and Circumstance's* spring poetry contest in 2013.
"Letter to My Son" received first prize for submissions to the *Dads of Disability* anthology
"Second Chance" received 2nd prize in the Urban Ocean Poetry Award in 2013 from the Long Beach Aquarium.
"October Wish" and "Night Visitors" won *The Painted Bride's* Sidecar prize in October and November of 2014 (respectively) and were published on the journal's website.

Contents

Part 1: Them

Fistulated Cow	11
Leavings	13
Binturong	14
Natural History	16
Feather and Flock	17
Epitaph	18
Second Chance	19
Sounding	20
Evolution	22
Succulents	23
Invader	25
Seal	26
What We Call Beautiful	27
Humane	28

Part 2: Us

Consolation	30
The Squeaky Wheel	31
Repair	34
Letter to My Son	35
Another Statistic	37
Fire	38
Apologies to Peter Bogdanovitch	39
Unenforceable	41
Mysteries	42
October Wish	44

Part 3: Me

Note to Self	47
8 Notes to Myself at Twenty	48
Labor Day	50

The Wrong Job	52
What I Remember	54
How to Get There	56
The Best Years of My Life	58
Valentine's Day	61
July	63
Summer Camp	64
Making Do	65
Swimming Lesson	67
Driving Lesson	69
Books Cannot Save Us	71
Secret	73
The Flyway	75

Part. 4: The Others

Notes of Earth's Diplomatic Liaison	79
The Ghost of an Ox Visits the Broken Yoke	81
Spring Fever	82
Medusa—An Unnatural History	83
Rebecca's Song	84
Hero	85
Sea Angel	86
The World to Come	87
Lemon	88
Night Visitors	89
Body Knowledge	90

About the Author

Part 1: Them

Fistulated Cow

> After a story on Radiolab, NPR

Beneath a shield of hide and flesh
the cow's stomach hangs
like a hammock from the triangular
scaffolding of the pelvis.
You've always guessed it was there
that alchemical apparatus
working away in the steamy darkness,

transmuting grass and hay
to silky curds, an ivory flow.
But now, you can see for yourself.
No need to hang back, to cower there
in a corner. Slip on those rubber gloves.
Enter the inner chamber.

We think of the stomach as a sack,
soft and loose as a pocket
in a much-laundered jacket.
It's more like a muscle.
Feel it grab your hand,
sucking the fingers down
into the vortex where intestines,
ribbed as a vacuum cleaner hose,
coil, and the sweet grass
travels the length of each helix,
each pearly arc, like tourists
queued at Disneyland, and the billions
of bugs do their work. And in you as well
the same mysterious everyday magic
you don't like to think about
goes on.

Now we'll put back the plug,
let the cow wade knee-high into a field of clover,
a body linked to other bodies,
making the most of the world.

Leavings

Whiff of a muskrat, many days gone
beneath the giant tires of a passing
eight-wheeler, all the delicate bits
broken, till feather-light,
printed with a palimpsest
of unreadable hieroglyphics.
What had once been
solid flesh aspires to air.
I pause on the road's shoulder
rapt as a videographer
seeing how it must have been:

First, the paunch split open,
spilling the bright guts.
The ribs, arched as a medieval
chapel, collapsed; then
the memorial procession began,
all those scavengers
worshiping at the shrine
of what was edible.
But once they had gathered
all they could, the carcass sagged,
an emptied burlap sack.
Now I ponder what is left, this being
the core strength of the much vaunted intellect.

Binturong

Penned in a pet store cage
so small he had no room
to turn around,
the binturong glowered—
bear cat, South Asian
resident of forests,
small time scavenger,
living on rodents and snails.

He seemed all burning eyes
and white incisors,
the incarnation of aggression,
curved claws as shiny
as the knobs on braided loaves,
as sharp as raptors' beaks.
His odor, not unlike the smell
of ripe socks in a gym,
rose in musky waves
above the heating vents,
assailed all visitors.

Not an appealing creature,
with his bristling whiskers,
coarse coat, sharp active snout,
something like a cross
between a badger and a cat—
long body, powerful short legs.
Yet for this pet-store owner,
the animal drew crowds,
mostly adolescents,
who poked at the mesh
and made faces,

as though savagery itself
were locked away
behind the flimsy wire.

Regardless of appearance,
binturongs are shy, reclusive.
This one snapped and snarled,
thrilling teenage girls.
The proprietor obliged,
throwing shreds of bloody
beef into the cage.

How shrewd
that pet store owner,
how cynical, to illustrate
the human animal
for what it was.

Natural History

In Philadelphia many years ago
even gypsy caterpillars seemed a cause
for celebration, and cabbage whites,
common as crab grass, almost like unicorns.
So when I saw a black swallowtail
drawn by an errant milkweed
in a sewer grate,
I stalked it with my net,
and finally caught it.
Bigger than my hand,
the splendid blue-black wings
folded and unfolded.
It lived for weeks on nectar from a tube,
beating those useless wings against the screen.

Feather and Flock

Consider the crow—alone
or among his fellows.
Shard of obsidian.
Splinter of night.
Like any intelligent being,
he bears all the weight
of ambivalence: at once
an eight-ball, atavistic
symbol of death,
cannibal and clown, both
vain and beautiful—
aware of the slick shine
of a blue-black back, beak
honed sharp on a branch,
fit to spear a songbird midair
or sing a crooked song.
All this, we claim, is hardwired
in the gut, the mind.
And yet, the bird is also
himself, so much more
than the gauche scavenger,
the cruel carnivore
we take him for.

Epitaph

Lonesome George is dead.
On tiny Pinto Island
in the Galapagos,
the only Giant Tortoise
of his kind left off
his bachelor
peregrinations
to stump into an afterlife
of all that's lost and gone.

He lived 100 years,
dodging sailors
and pirates bent
on turtle stew
and then a crew
of naturalists
to be the last
lonely survivor.
Now he's gone.

In his memory,
a flotilla of clouds
flies in formation.

Second Chance

The sea lions on the wharf
at Newport mug for tourists,
batting their lashes,
begging for a bit of bait.

For their part, the tourists,
in their deck shoes and Prada,
stroll the bayside paths
or glide by in rented yachts.

Today, the ocean too,
in its ancient innocence,
is tricked out to attract,
lying on its back
like a gray cat, plume tail
curling around the curve
of the harbor, playing nice.

But in the next big storm,
the sea will roar,
sweep away the shops
and paths, the bumper cars
and geegaws with gigantic
claws, clearing it all away.

Sounding

Because our human ears are not made
for hearing underwater, we once believed
that whales and other creatures of the sea
must occupy a still and solemn world,
some perfect scene beneath a crystal globe.
Somehow, we overlooked the borborygmic
belch of sea floor tremors, cracking sea ice,
the songs of whales. Now
we realize the hush of rain
might lull the dozing dolphins.
We've heard the calls of creatures
once thought dumb, and know
it isn't only cows and sheep that low or bleat,
but toadfish, seals, and urchins.
Even the seahorse makes a sound
like knocking on a hollow wooden door.

The ocean's loud as a metropolis.
Yet once we add our sonar
to the mix, technology we took
from bats and whales,
it can render some cetaceans deaf,
shut down their inner GPS, and leave them
beached in hundreds on the shore.
Proliferating cargo ships,
their groaning engines droning ever louder,
often mute the bellows of sperm whales,
keeping them from finding mates.

The ocean is itself, not a place
that we imagine. No silent sunlit dome,
where creatures sway to music just beyond the ear,
but a home, and part of our own world,
prey to all its problems, all its cruelty, color, awe.
Same sky, same stars, yet singing its own song.

Evolution

The night-blooming cereus,
Queen of the Desert, perfumes the yard,
giving her one-night-only performance.
Everyone knows this show for what it is:
an effort to employ olfactory wiles
in service of the seed, attracting
avid Sphynx moths and bats,
metallic scarabs like bouncers
in their glittering regalia.
A scent strong as a snare,
tangible as the bug-eyed peepers'
insistent shrilling in the sodden leaves.

For a week, the bud hung heavy, until
just yesterday it began to turn
up toward the light, green bodice
beginning to swell, as the double
flower prepared to meet its suitors.
Fully open now, it holds itself out
to be tasted, petals a cupped palm
nestled in a jagged ruff of lower leaves,
crowned by a yellow starburst.
As I watch, a moth's proboscis
unfurls like a fiddlehead.

Before morning, the flower will wither,
and the moon too deflate
like a day-old helium balloon.
I too play a role, as surely
smitten as the moth or beetle,
the peepers, compelled to stitch a song
out of the perfumed air.

Succulents

Creatures of adversity,
though born of want,
arise in many
shapes and colors—
bulbous barrel cactus,
barbed with golden thorns,
dark green Euphorbia ,
white-seamed along
the tall, thornless stalks,
Echeveria, swirling
like galaxies,
waxy purple-gray
and green corsages
spreading out
across the ground—
bred in the desert's
brief season.

No gardener, I learned
their names and how
to recognize the cause
of root rot, when to repot,
how to propagate
new plants—tiny leaflets
rising from cut leaves,
relics of distant deserts
in my living room,
on my lawn.

They taught me
how to thrive
out of my proper place,

rising in weak sunlight,
chalky soil,
how to take
the little that I had,
making it more than suffice,
learning from living rocks,
translucent windows
bringing sunlight to the root,
enough to bloom.

Invader

All winter, this Phaleopsis orchid,
domesticated in its plastic pot,
sits astride the kitchen sink,
back to the window blind,
staring like a prisoner.

Fuchsia and cream, reticulated
as a topographical map, its rivers
and its plains, the purple-veined
bodies in an anatomical atlas,
It has known only
the scented air of a hothouse,
the steam and stink of simulated tropics.

But after months of dormancy,
the flowers slowly turn
their blank,
abstracted faces
toward the light.

One flowering spike
spirals the window frame,
climbing up and up
toward the high ceiling.
External roots snake everywhere,
turning everything they touch to jungle.
Rubbery tendrils probe the recalcitrant
knife block, red plastic dish drainer,
bottle of Palmolive liquid, searching
for succor they can never find.
Yet fueled by sunlight, the plant
escapes the boundaries
of my human world.

Seal

Clearly these mammals have imagination.
I watched one spin in place,
eyes closed, as I did once at five,
falling in a dizzy heap to watch
the room spin, the familiar
turning alien, but quickly taking shape
again within accustomed walls.
The seal though kept its eyes
shut tight, a meditative whirling
like a sufi's dance. His eyelids
never quivered as he spun,
bobbing a bit in the enclosure,
calm face composed,
resembling a dead pharaoh
wrapped tight within his gold
sarcophagus, entering
the next world, dreaming
a life relentless as the tides.

What We Call Beautiful

Not every creature that flies
can be a Lyrebird,
extravagant tail trailing
the ground, within reach
of the naturalist's greedy
net, the predator's claws.

We can say the same of
the pale green Luna moth,
the size of a melon, and echoing
a melon's musky scent,
Chinese lantern on the night's
indelible surface,
or the splendid macaw:
imagine palm trees
full of their loud brightness.

All of these flaunt their flash
under the ordinary moon,
the sun worn out with shining.

In all of this, who notices
the starling's black-rimmed
yellow eyes, as bright
as any flame, or the geometer moth,
brown wings patterned with the maps
of unknown continents?

Yet under the microscope's
loupe of light, even
the wing of a cabbage white
vibrates, luminous
as the most exquisite plumage.

Humane

> To biologist, Susan Simard

Can you tell the forest from the tree?
I used to think so. But now
I know it isn't possible.
Everything that seems
only itself is really not.

The giant redwood,
emblem of the individual,
in truth makes up a part
of something even larger
we can't see. In the dark, the roots
reach out their bone-white fingers,
not just taking from the earth
to serve themselves, as we expect,
but giving gifts of nitrogen
to all the other trees around.

Species and kind are not an issue.
And all this time, we've seen
only ourselves reflected
on the world's blank screen.
So when we finally climb out
on the Martian dust, how likely
that we'll recognize the welcome there,
a subtle perturbation of the airless sky?

Part 2: Us

Consolation

> To Linda Dann, on the loss of her husband

You must ride this train to the very
last stop, though you will feel tempted
to disembark when the windows fill
with that awful light, the world insisting,
going on as always, and the eucalyptus,
all in a row, standing like sorrowful sisters.
Do we go to our friends, to words,
for consolation, to be told our fears are imagined,
that the darkness under the door
can be easily dispelled, or to walk together
at the last into the breach?

The Squeaky Wheel

My mother—pretty, prim,
never flashy—turned out
in her white gloves for Saturdays
at Wanamakers, downtown.
She taught me to eat lunch only
in places with white tablecloths,
cloth napkins, and the hum
of quiet conversation,
and corrected my infelicitous
grammar, gleaned from playmates
on the grubby streets of Philadelphia.
For this I belatedly thank her,
though she kept her imagination
buttoned up against uncivil
thoughts, tried unsuccessfully
to censor mine as well.

It must have been hard
to have been married
to my father, king
of wherever he was,
who embodied such drama,
dark brows lowered,
ready for a storm.

He mocked her manners
and her haughty bearing,
the perfect enunciation
that made her so conspicuous
despite herself.
Yet she never said a word,
except under her breath,
and then only in Afrikaans.

I used to love to watch her
pouring tea for smiling
women friends, high priestess
of civility, but they would never
come more than one time.
My father drove them off,
and then the silver tea
service and cutlery she'd bought
in London were retired.
She polished them
in silence, or else recited
tales of former glory as she rubbed,
as though her efforts
might restore the past.
Soon, no one would listen
when she spoke.
I'd heard it all before.

My father simply
told her to shut up.
She stopped singing,
telling stories of her family
in South Africa, and slipped
away, into her private world.

So when at 93, her mind
half gone, she let me see
the jealousy she felt
at the attention her husband
always got from everyone—
caregivers propping up his pillows,
polishing his shoes, doctors
laughing at his jokes
and jotting notes about

his special, complicated case—
it spoke a lifetime of missed chances,
regret that she, so charming
and popular in youth,
had been reduced to this woman,
pointing with a pink-tipped finger.
"Doctors want to see
me too," she said,
turning away.

Repair

Writing something is almost as hard as making a table
—Gabriel Garcia Marquez

For my father

Coal-heaver, caulker, yeoman, your almanac
predicted a warm spring. City-bred,
you nonetheless planted what you had
in the ready earth. Your hands
knew their place, always at work,
repairing the television, rewiring the lamp.
How disappointed you were to see
I was not the offspring you hoped for,
so clumsy was I and inept with every tool
except the pen, always reading and dreaming.
It's much too late to justify my character.
Millions of years of genetic history has brought us here,
to this faulty mechanism that cannot be mended.

Letter to My Son

How could we know at first
that anything was wrong? You were
the only baby we had cared for up till then.
When you cried for hours at a time
and couldn't stop, despite
our efforts to appease, to feed,
rock, bathe, and change,
we thought that this must simply
be the way of babies, the part
that no one mentioned in the books.

And after all, you were
so perfect, dark eyes fringed
as a flower, starfish hand
splayed in my palm, but as you grew,
"terrible two" went on for years.
You wouldn't eat, seldom slept,
bending nature to your will.
At first, the doctors found no problem.
Sometimes I wondered if we might
just be imagining, hoped it was so.

I would watch you race around
the house, your face almost
a double of my own at four or five,
superhero cape streaming behind
a paradigm of movement.
Sometimes I'd hold you upside down
just to still you for a moment,
and we'd both laugh and laugh
at that vain gesture. And sometimes
your rage would suddenly surprise me

when a favorite game had to end
or the bath had grown too cold
or my energy would simply flag.
Where did a child that small
gather all that strength? And yet
I wouldn't have you other than you are.
Let the world absorb your energy
and your will bend others always
toward the good. What seems to be
infirmity can prove a gift.

Another Statistic

She could have been someone
I knew, this girl on the train platform,
someone I saw years ago,
riding the Frankfort El.
She never smiled, dark eyes
scanning the miles of track
and wires, the river,
never a human face,
hair curling around her
shoulders like smoke.
As she walked the empty streets,
graffitied names swelled on the walls,
the throats of tree frogs,
bellowing their territorial song.
Backed into the bricked-off
alleys and courtyards,
she couldn't see the way out,
the ladders and fire escapes.
She took another route,
the melancholy path
through the woods
from which she never returned—
dark spot in the winter grass,
touched with frost.
She could have been me,
but she wasn't.

Fire

From a line in a book review taken from The Sweet Girl,
A novel by Annabel Lyon, on All Things Considered, NPR

We must all have fire in us
Breathing out prodigious clouds of smoke
On winter mornings, when the windows frost.

And this goes on for years, as though
Nothing at all were lost.
We must have fire in us.

And where the gangly palms outnumber oaks
Overheated sleepers make a tangle of the sheets
Dreaming of winter mornings when the windows frost.

Who can calculate the cost
Of burning so steadily and long?
We must have fire in us

Or else we'd be reduced to ash and ends
Far sooner than we are.
We must have fire in us
To brave those winter mornings when the windows frost.

Apologies to Peter Bogdanovitch

> With borrowings from a review by that author published
> in the *New York Times Book Review*

I have always loved old movies,
savoring their texture, silver-gray
frames corrugated with slips
and cracks, skips in the sound track
a rosary of intentional error
I trace each devoted time.
How is it that my eyes have never
craved a flash of seductive
turquoise (distant pool or oasis)?
Or the olive-green highlights
in the ingénue's white-blond hair?
Instead, I am thrilled each iteration
by the characters carved in obsidian
against a nacreous sky.
Maybe I like all these subtleties
left to the imagination, film being
much less literal than it seems,
the art of the indeterminate.

I embrace the old Hollywood
so lately a cow town, self-conscious
chorus girl putting on airs,
so much more than the modern
one, worn with pretending,
desolate as last year's tinsel.
And what about the iconic
movie star and his director?
Didn't they both grow up
during the so-called silent era—
though we knew it was never

actually silent, with at least
a piano or often a full orchestra,
and all those sound effects?

Unenforceable

After an interview on The World, *NPR*

In Istanbul, "forbidden" is forbidden.
For censors in that city, words
are things and things are dangerous:
"canals" conceal back passageways.
"Hot" and "teens" are banished,
yet children still grow older,
summer still persists.

Though words for that or this
may disappear, the body speaks in code,
communicates what custom can't deny.
Censors and lexicographers despair:
"forbidden" makes its home in all the tender
folds between the fingers, no matter that
in Istanbul, "forbidden" is forbidden.

Mysteries

It's no wonder people crave them:
in these orderly worlds,
human intellect's the star,
borne by whatever
personage we can imagine:
prim British spinster,
medieval monk,
rabbi or genial priest,
well-upholstered African,
wise-cracking private eye.

They notice every clue
disguised as random accident,
possess uncanny intuition
and a streak of paranoia
wide as a six-lane highway,
uncovering week after weary week
the corpses that keep turning up
in multiples of three or more.
One wonders that these villages
and towns were not unpeopled long ago.

No end of novel ways to buy the farm—
eaten by pigs, dispatched
with a shovel, poisoned
with an untraceable elixir—
all gleefully presented
on the page or screen.
At once disturbing and delightful.

Why is it that events that would be
horrid if we saw them on the news
inspire another sort of thrill

in a film or book or Sunday afternoon
amusement? Perhaps because
the formula we know so well assures us
the perpetrator will be found
will suffer retribution
while the world itself
scarcely offers any guarantee.

Freud argued that our dreams
fulfill our deepest wishes,
even when it seems more likely
they reflect our fears.
It's true that we're a mystery,
especially to ourselves.
Oedipus discovered
what we don't want to admit:
we might be the criminals we seek.
with a shovel, poisoned
with an untraceable elixir—
all gleefully presented
on the page or screen.
At once disturbing and delightful.

Why is it that events that would be
horrid if we saw them on the news
inspire another sort of thrill
in a film or book or Sunday afternoon
amusement? Perhaps because
the formula we know so well assures us
the perpetrator will be found
and will suffer retribution
while the real world
scarcely offers any guarantee.

October Wish

What would it be like
pocketing this early fall sunlight,
to empty it by the bucketful
into a winter sky,
white as the frozen ground?

Or to save every elegant blossom
on the orchid's now-bare stalk,
to send another surging
from its spot?

If I could shape the world,
so full of sadness and loss,
parse it like a phrase,
could alphabetize its confusion
until it resolved to sense,
making meaning last.

Part 3: Me

Note to Self

You may not know me,
but I once was you.
Together at the window,
we'd grow dizzy, watching
the swirling snowflakes
settle into five foot drifts.
At school, I whispered
answers in your ear, and all
the questions teachers
didn't want to hear.
I read over your shoulder
the books we both loved best,
told you how to catch
the tiger swallowtail
that beat its patterned
wings against the pane.
You once fell off your bicycle
into broken glass; but it is I
who bear the scar.
Like you, I have a kind of
power born of shame.
At eleven, you began to bleed.
But when you asked her why,
mother embraced, then slapped you,
passing down the ancient curse.
I haven't seen you since,
although for years I'd haunt
the empty pool, the park,
the library, all the places
where you used to go.
I am you now,
with a difference.
There are questions
only you can answer.

8 Notes to Myself at Twenty

Telling the future is simple
when one speaks to the past.
I send this missive to my
twenty-year-old self,
telling her nothing
is going to be easy,
taking her hands,
too soft for any
good purpose.

I know she will not listen.
See how she looks at me,
thinking I must be mad,
like the women on the bus
or street corners with
their baggy coats, smeared
lipstick, sharing their crazy
wisdom with whomever
will listen. She doesn't
see how my face mirrors hers
as I lean in, predicting
what has already happened.

I tell her: You will
face everything you fear
and survive it.
You will make the same
mistakes for years, suffer
the same consequences—
a song you have sung
every day of your life
and still not quite learned.

A penny-ante prophet,
I will advise her:
Pay attention!
Observe the moon
in all of its phases.
Learn the names of trees.
Eat the ripest fruit.

Labor Day

It wasn't my first job,
the one at the aquarium store,
just the one that stuck.
Once there was only
a man with a net,
a few sparse tanks
of mollies and swordtails,
bowls of fighting fish
in their elegant silks
eying each other through the glass.

By the time I turned eighteen,
an army of salespeople
patrolled the aisles.
In the two-hundred-gallon display,
triggerfish like African masks
picked at algae with their striped teeth,
orange anemones carpeted
the bottom of the tank.

Death was a regular
part of the job,
filling, then emptying
gallon bags of dead fish,
floating on the surface of the tanks.

I learned something every day
about cleaning aquariums
full of electric eels,
how to catch that one
elusive guppy
among hundreds,

learned also about myself
as I bent over the koi pool
with my net, looking for
the one with blue fins,
distracted by
my own reflection.

Chafing at being merely
a willing pair of hands,
I wanted more,
couldn't keep quiet
if customers
or bosses
were wrong.
I never changed,
whatever job I was doing—
still telling people
what they didn't
want to hear.

The Wrong Job

It must have been
my doppelganger
they were thinking of,
when the counselor advised me
I ought to be a funeral director.

As I saw it, I didn't
fit the profile:
grave downcast eyes,
voice well-suited to a dirge,
all minor keys and monotone,
teeth set like headstones
in a florid face.

I couldn't bludgeon
grieving daughters
or nervous sons
with false good nature,
sympathy-for-profit,
leading them
up and down long rows
of coffins, tricked out
to look like satin-lined convertibles,
bargain urns, fashioned of
sturdy cardboard, yet capable
of sheltering those heavy
bits of gristle, bone, and ash
just long enough to bury
or scatter on the waves.

Now, although I'm glad
I didn't go in that direction,

I know it's certainly unfair
to judge a whole profession
by its worst.
Since death is part of life,
some people, like some animals,
must have a role
in cleaning up what's left,
tending to ritual,
allowing the rest of us
to turn our faces
toward the light
and walk away.

What I Remember

*Home is the place where, when you have to go there,
they have to take you in.*
—Robert Frost

It should have been my sanctuary,
but for me, "home" meant
the place I fled—repeatedly.

It wasn't just my narrow house
but all the others too, attached
like sisters at the sash, the patch
of lawn and double flights of stairs
fronting a one-way street.

Every window had its pair of eyes,
every stoop its seated guardian,
high up on patios, like jurors.
One day I passed before them,
sticky ice pop clenched
hard between my fingers.

The smallest child, younger than I,
lisped my name, threw a buzzing
jar of bees into my face,
proclaiming me "Bug Lady,"
to general hilarity—glass everywhere.
At first I cried, like anyone
wanting to be liked, but soon
their calls lost meaning,
more like cicadas' shrill vibrations
than human words.

Alone at the window, I'd watch
snow blanketing the brown
uneven stubble, rendering it
almost beautiful,
as the garden's last leavings
(hard green tomatoes, rose hips
swollen as a chilblained thumb)
dissolved to dust beneath a dimpled drift.

New neighbors took the place of old.
Their eyes were just as hard.
Shades pulled tight, even
in summer, keeping the heat inside.

Years later, when my father
had a stroke and mother's mind
had slipped away,
no one stopped me on the street
to say hello or ask where I had been.
I still haunt those streets,
but only in my dreams.

How to Get There

For Phyllis Schmulenson and the Bushrod Library

First, find yourself in Philadelphia.
Travel the rutted highway,
hair-trigger Roosevelt Blvd.,
America's most hazardous road,
with its faint odor of Oreos
from the Nabisco plant.
There you'll see the empty basin
of the swimming pool
where I once swam, or tried to,
in the shallow end—just a concrete
gully now, full of weeds.
Turn right on Devereaux, passing
row homes, people watching, wary,
from the stoops, the corner
where the synagogue burned.
Turn right on Castor Avenue
and left on Stirling. You've reached
your destination; park.

This is—and isn't—where it started,
here at the Bushrod Library.
I knew the books much better
than I did my neighbors.
Worn paperbacks, in their creaky
metal rack, new books.
It all looks different now.
Where the magazines
once stood, computers.
Someone new where
Miss Schmulenson,
the librarian, once

handed me the world,
volumes in all colors, of all sorts.
False eyelashes askew,
enthusiastic hands
molding the air,
she thrilled me with her tales
of demonstrations, Israel,
studies at the university,
Where ever you are, Phyllis,
I have done those things
and more. You gave me
zest enough to share,
inspired me to shape
the world I saw,
to pass it all along.

The Best Years of My Life

The building seemed more factory
than school—square and black,
windows covered with dark paper
that willfully shut out
what light there was.
I'd walk those endless corridors
past adolescent boys
who prodded breasts with pins,
thinking them false (they weren't),
girls peering sideways through
hair blessedly long and straight,
while mine corkscrewed out of control.

Lunchtimes were worse.
Every day she'd wait for me
next to the dining room.
A good 100 pounds
heavier than I,
she'd toss me down the stairs
into the trash,
among the milk cartons.
I'd wish that I could fight her,
but all I had was wits,
and words just made her
punch me harder when bystanders
laughed at her expense.
Those bystanders were worse
than she was: the security guard,
amused, smoking his illicit
cigarette as he leaned
against the wall,
the students eager

for the regularly scheduled
wrestling match,
featuring oddball contenders:
me, standing 4'8,"
her, looming like a helium
balloon in a parade,
the benign made awful
by being so much out of scale,
her eyebrows bat-black arches
on a painted face, pale mask
against the darker complexion
of her neck.

The principal just said
it was my problem.
My parents shook their heads,
saying that tattletales would get
no sympathy from them.
And so I spent each lunchtime
for a year in the girl's bathroom,
afraid to venture out beyond the door
until the bell rang.
Fitting nowhere, I fought
to transfer to another school,
but in the end,
I stayed there, miserable
and angry, wishing I could
beat back hostility,
or worse, indifference
with my guts or grace.
As always, I just had to wait.

Long past leaving,
I held on to rage,
although it burned me
like a rope wound tight
around my chest.
Yet thinking of it now,
I feel the odd sensation
of compassion for my batterer,
cast out and alone,
suffering her private hell
as I did mine.

Valentine's Day

February was a red month
when I was ten, though frost
patterned the pane
and heaps of dull gray
snow cluttered the walk.

For weeks, I'd gather up
my crimson forces—
construction paper,
doilies, red ribbons,
glitter, and the rest,
reflecting on the heart.

I knew the organ in my chest
looked nothing like the
rounded two-winged circles
I would cut with careful
scissors, though the real one
had its double-chambers too,
veins like ribbons, beating
a tattoo all day and night.
Was this knot of flesh really
home to the affections
or just a bit of meat
like the chicken hearts
I'd spoon from mother's soup?

I struggled to imagine all the heat
the heart was fabled to inspire.
I loved my dog, my parents,
my best friend, afternoons
spent at the window, book open
on my lap. I even eyed the fellow

down the block, but couldn't
fathom how that simple pump
could prime not just one
body, but all of life,
love, but also jealousy
and hate, because such feelings
can't be pried apart.

What did these paper stand ins
really signify? Not much.
And yet, I hoped for one
from every kid in class.
At ten, Valentine's a recess
for the heart—all the sweetness,
nothing of experience—the sting.

July

A summer night, just like the ones
I remember, when the ice cream truck
circled the block like a recurrent dream,
and distant thunder rumbled
and sometimes the rain
poured down, then stopped
all at once, rising in clouds like nebulae,
so humid quarters stuck to my palm
in hot red circles.

No wonder I couldn't sleep
with the moths blundering
into the screen and desperate
signals of lovelorn fireflies
outside my window
and the laughter of neighbors
the red ends of their cigarettes
burning holes in the sky like sparklers
the murmur of the ballgame
rising from a hundred transistor radios
on and on into the night.

Summer Camp

I was eleven and had never been to camp.
Being poor at sports, I stayed at home and read,
bagging swallowtails and minnows,
lightning bugs in bottles, dying stars.

That year, my parents shipped me off
to be the only stranger in the bunk.
I didn't miss my home, but camp
was not congenial—cold pool at morning,
powdered eggs. The others
locked me naked outside the cabin,
no towel to shield me, nowhere to hide.

I spent my evenings singing Dylan
with the counselor, days feeding rabbits
at the nature center, while the others
fielded softballs. Of all the sports,
only archery seemed interesting, although
I couldn't draw the bow. On Friday nights,
I sang the Shabbat prayers.

Sassafras and tulip trees quivered
in the breeze, bright moss a mingled
carpet at my feet. And there I met
two artists, happy in their lives,
their A-frame house deep in the woods
where paintings covered every wall.
This gave me hope: Somewhere
there were people like myself.

Making Do

I learned the art of making do
from parents who excelled at this—
ingenious at devising ways to live
rarely straining meager means.

I didn't wear the brand-name
clothes I coveted, my seamstress
mother stitching, my father
tinkering with wires and water pipes,
meticulous and focused.

Books came from the library
and the Chevy had no power
brakes or air conditioning.
Fridays, dad would drop
a silver dollar in my bank;
later, these would pay for college.

Saturday, we'd sup on *gribines*
smeared on warm rye—
soft yellow chicken fat
with onion cracklings.
The *pushkah* in the kitchen
filled with nickels, pennies,
meant for people
whose needs were greater
than our own.
My father planted radishes
and roses on our patch of lawn.

And yet at Christmas we'd drive out
to snowy suburbs, making a tour
of graceful houses, looking
through picture windows
garlanded with light, where
families gathered by the tree,
its wrapped and ribboned packages,
all in a Technicolor halo
the television cast on this
crèche of the American dream.

Swimming Lesson

I used to love the pool's perfect blue,
watching the others in their too-tight
swimsuits tied at the neck
jump into the cool water all at once
instead of one toe at a time, like me.

I loved the water so much,
I didn't want to spoil it by swimming,
disturbing the smooth surface
with my kicking legs.
I preferred to sit
on the slippery edge
sifting water through my fingers.

But once I climbed in,
lowering my face to look
under the surface
at the blue-tiled bottom
of the pool, I loved
the way the water
rippled with secret light.

Everything was fine,
until the water rose
inch by inch
 up to my shoulders,
my neck, and over my nose.
My feet thrashed,
nothing solid beneath them,
and I forgot all the lessons.
Panic filled me
as a balloon fills up with air,

stretching till the thin skin,
almost translucent, bursts.

My teacher called out, "Float!"
but her voice sounded
so far away.
Up became down.
Drawn to the blue
perfection of the bottom,
where phantom light wavered,
I dived down and down.
When the lifeguard
grabbed me by the arm
and hauled me out,
I was almost sorry.

Driving Lesson

Every Sunday afternoon for years
I'd face the hour that I dreaded
all week long: a driving lesson
with my father.
Like all fifteen-year-olds,
I wanted to grow up,
and driving was the proof
that I was grown.
I longed to get into the car
and go, no more asking
for a ride or taking buses.

My father's car, a dowdy Chevy,
poked like a pontoon
along cracked streets
where neighbors sat outside
brick bungalows on lawn chairs,
sneering as we rolled slowly by.
And truthfully, it must have been a sight.
My feet hardly reached the pedals,
however augmented with blocks
or phone books. If I slid down,
I couldn't see the street.
No power steering either:
I had to fight the car to make it turn
and backing up was hopeless.

But if the car itself were not enough,
there was my father—grim gargoyle,
full of fury, grabbing fistfuls of my hair
or stomping on my feet, as others
sped by, windows up, faces
averted, pretending not to see.
In winter we would glide down snowy

hills by Tookany to visit cousins, or stop
at the aquarium. My father made me
strip off boots and socks and drive
barefooted, toes frozen
to the pedal, body stiff with fear.

The lesson always ended the same way,
when dad would reach his rigid arm
across the seat, open the door,
motion me out, two miles from home.
Pulling on my shoes and socks,
I'd muse on the ineffable, full of sorrow
at what could not be said,
watching the nascent moon,
translucent blot on the pink sky,
rise slowly as I walked.

We wouldn't talk
from one week to the next,
but when next Sunday came around,
I'd hope things might be different,
climb into the car, attempt
a starchy smile, and try again.

Books Cannot Save Us

In the very center of the living room,
my father sat, a sentinel,
and watched the news.
Even if he fell asleep, I didn't dare
to turn the channel or switch off the set.
I never knew when he'd explode,
and off would come the belt.

Like any prey, I knew enough to flee.
I'd run downstairs, wet laundry
on the indoor clothesline
slapping at my arms,
to reach the door.
Nowhere to go, even
once I turned the balky lock.
Should I head down Stirling
to the playground,
or up the avenue, my father
roaring in my wake?

No one would help.
I knew I'd pay the price—
for what, I wasn't sure,
would have to bear the belt,
and worse, his screaming face,
veins bulging like an ivy vine
squeezing a tree to death.

Once he caught me,
as he always did, I'd
cast about for strategies.
Once I threw myself

across the room,
by the aquarium,
where the bookshelf stood,
filled with *Aesop's Fables,*
Mother Goose, *The Encyclopedia
of Tropical Fishes.*

I grabbed a few of these,
shoved them down my pants,
so when he hit me,
he would hit the books.
But they only made it worse,
thumping hard against my thighs
and leaving Technicolor bruises
on my skinny hips.

I knew the books I read
would have a similar effect
because I never would
escape into a looking glass
or wardrobe, would have to wait
for years until I left.
And yet, these books
gave me instruction—how to live
a life where drama could be art
and pain might be allayed
by the very act of writing it all down.

Secret

Between my mother's legs,
a barbed-wire tangle,
nothing like Barbie's,
an unmapped territory
I hadn't traveled to
just yet, where I didn't want to go.

I didn't have a Ken doll,
but I'd seen the zebras
at the zoo, black penis growing
and growing, like Pinocchio's nose.
And I'd seen my father too.
Every morning he'd take me
and my mother to the shower,
make us strip, and soap us up
under the spray, let the hot water
wash us clean.

This went on till at eleven,
well-developed for my age,
I wasn't smooth like Barbie anymore.
We were visiting the 64 World's Fair,
staying with a family friend,
a child psychiatrist,
who stopped us in the hall
as we trooped, in towels, to the shower.

Her eyebrows rose and rose.
She grabbed me by the shoulders,
shoved me hard into the bathroom
by myself, and slammed the door.
The hot water stung my scalp.

Through the steam,
I heard her shrill voice
outside the bathroom door,
but not the words,
and wondered what I'd done.

From that time on, we never
saw that family friend again.
I stuffed all the keyholes with toilet paper,
showered alone,
ashamed of what I'd become.

The Flyway

Long ago, when I was almost
grown, my father, saying
nothing of our destination,
took me to a forlorn spot—
under a bridge
between two busy roads.
We pulled off to the side,
on the soft dirt shoulder.
He pointed up
into a gray, uncertain sky.

A river of birds, its edges
delineated as if with a ruler,
filled the windows,
the honking of Canada geese,
calls of countless songbirds,
endless flapping of wings,
breakers on some far-off shore--
all of these birds somehow
going in the same direction,
knowing where they needed to be.

We stood a long time,
wondering at this emptying
of every bird there was
into the elsewhere.
It grew too dark to watch,
yet the flight continued.

Bound to a cycle of our own,
we silently slipped back
into the car and headed home.

Part. 4: The Others

Notes of Earth's Diplomatic Liaison

I chose a public servant's life despite
the narrow desk-bound days this choice
suggests, a life late to the carnival,
totting up my sums and signing forms
every day, including weekends.
Yet this job isn't precisely what I feared:
witness the startled plumbers
at the Plaza when the ambassador
from a planet I won't name gets indigestion.
Let's just say that earthly plumbing
wasn't made for that. Or explaining
to the manager of Disney Hall
that pianos seem a proper place
for certain species to repose.
Sometimes I think how pleasant
it would be to go back to my former post
where fixing traffic tickets was the norm
and every client had a human face like mine.
Instead, I face the daily sad surprise
of puzzling out the residue on walls,
apologizing till the solemn smile
sticks to my face. Boring it's not.
I can't help but admire the great diversity—
as various as any garden, Buddha bellies,
arms like tongs, the many eyes of Delex Minor,
species perforated as kitchen colanders or
smooth unfeatured spheres emitting light.
If these were humans coping with an alien
world, we'd doubtless breach the deepest
taboos, never meaning to offend.
So, when fielding calls, I advise
we stifle our dismay or scorn as though

the future of our world depended on it—
as well it might. And while we're at it, forgiving
might work best among the human tribe as well.

The Ghost of an Ox Visits the Broken Yoke

After a painting by Clive Hicks Jenkins

This is where it happened,
where the ox fell in his traces,
where stars cluster
like seeds strewn in the dark .

All those years he never looked up,
drawing the curved blade through the field,
uprooting yarrow and clover,
sweet green grass, damp with dew.

Not even his arched ribs remain,
the prow of a beached ship,
the rude yoke lying broken forever,
young wheat rising.

Stately and pale, shorn of his heavy body,
his crescent horns moon white,
the ox stands like a god or an actor
in a red pool of light,
returning for one last look
before joining the herd, a constellation
of cattle grazing in the gray distance.

Spring Fever

O April with its soiled
shorts, its giddy sunshine!
On the hillside, blushing purple
as eczema on afflicted cheeks,
the bees again are gathering
their golden riches, excavating
the hairy slopes of orchids,
glamorous as Amazons.
Chaste as grain still fattening
in the field, they dedicate
their lives to a hive of identical
others, while grubs wait,
sealed into pristine cubicles
until a sister nursemaid carefully
uncorks them. Perhaps it is
the promise of the briefest
sip of nectar, more nuanced
than the most expensive spirits
and with a kick stronger than absinthe
that fuels this species-wide philanthropy.
Are these creatures made
more virtuous than we?
That explains it: they are
the angels we've heard so much
about, armed with swords,
winged, industrious,
and far from human.

Medusa—An Unnatural History

Poor girl, always losing
your head, sucker
for the sharp sting
of momentary passion.
The sea god saw you
walking by the shore,
and claimed you,
drawing you farther
and farther out to sea,
a boat without a rudder
or a sail.

You were lithe and elegant then,
beautiful as the surf,
golden curls flowing
down your back,
but bound to the goddess at birth,
promising to remain
chaste and cold
as the marble maiden
drawing her bow
on the temple portico.

All these years hence,
you have returned
to the subtle sea
carried at its will,
shimmering circle
of protoplasm,
fringed with tentacles,
riding the night-blue waves.

Rebecca's Song

Meditation on *Toldot,* Genesis 25:19-28.9

So long have I been barren,
like these dun-colored hills,
parched and bare, that now
the very rocks erupt
with blossoms bright as blood
on the shocked sand.
Now that my womb is full,
I hardly know where to stand.

In ushering two nations
through these narrow gates
I teach that all our enemies
are also brothers,
all enemies ourselves.
Turning one son against the other
I steal advantage from the stingy earth,
gaining gold from the generosity
of my own palm.

Hero

> After I Need a Hero, an episode of *RadioLab*

From a "position of safety,"
The hero acts, without fear
or a thought for self-preservation.
She sees someone in danger,
does what she must,
preserves a life.

This one left his daughters
on a subway platform
because a voice he didn't
recognize assured him
he'd be safe. He leaped
onto the tracks, and when
he couldn't lift the victim,
shielded that person so
the train passed safely over both.

Another man, sprung barefoot
from his bed, pulled three
unconscious victims from a burning
car, while silent neighbors watched
him from the side and wouldn't help.
The Greeks believed that heroes
bear the blood of deities.
But another model
of the deity suggests
all humans have this in them.
Weak and flawed, yet full
of will that can be bent
to any purpose, good or ill.

Sea Angel

For the Bedouin, scanning the impermanent
landscape of sand from the back
of a swaying camel, the sea is an angel.
The desert extends to the shore, sandstone
escarpments gradually giving way to waves,
so similar in form they might have been poured
from the same mold, fine red sand
and the bluest water imaginable,
tantalizing but undrinkable,
refusing to take any form for long.

On the darkest night in the Negev,
the shepherd senses the caracal
and hyena, the subtle rustle of the viper.
The dunes dream of lying once more
at the bottom of an ancient sea.
Far away, the surf rises,
arched wings of the angel,
messenger of the desert God,
whose silence contains everything.

The World to Come

Under the ground, the seventeen-year locusts wait.
Their oversized eyes take in everything
though there is little to see
until they rise from the ground
like seraphim, their jointed legs
twitching a jig to the pleasure of movement.
Thick as thumbs, each one launches
its body into the improbable air, where
they meet one another for the first and last time,
leaving only husks behind.

Lemon

I have heard we are all
just extravagant instruments
of the gustatory urge, made
to transport it to the nearest
source of nourishment—
an orchard of peaches
perhaps, still rock hard nubbins
at the base of embryonic blooms,
or an aquarium stocked with a school
of silver-sided tuna behind bright glass.
I awake in my round bed in the center
of everything that is, the room a yellow
wedge fragrant as summer and as bright.
How, in fact, have I managed to sleep
in all this brightness? On these soft
yellow feathers full of liquid
like a canary without a song?

Night Visitors

The dead do not remember
who they were.
Their feelings, fractured
in the fall from flesh,
are not the same,
glances glacial,
words few, dismissive.
It would take a locksmith
to make the tumblers fall into place
and let the doors swing
free again between us.

Life swaddles us in plush,
in all the rich distractions
of the world—morning
breaths and sunset signals.
But once they've gone,
the dead see only
tied-off ends, the underside,
and not the patterns.
No wonder they're disgruntled,
sundered from these riches,
gaining access only through our dreams.

Body Knowledge

    For Lavina Blossom

I used to think the hands
knew nothing, faithful tools,
feeling around in the earth,
flexing the versatile thumb.

I knew the hands could feel
the texture of bark, the tip
of the kitchen's sharpest
knife, yet called this
dumb sensation, without sense.

But with focus, the fingertips
can find a dime in a pocket
full of change, can learn
what year it was minted.

The blind can read a book
or tell the time by touch.
The clever hands of lovers
find out the other's secret places.

Clearly, the hands can close
the circuit between body
and mind, can draw a line,
can write lines too, like this.

About the Author

Robbi Nester lives and writes in Southern California. She is the author of a chapbook, *Balance* (White Violet, 2012) and a collection of poems, *A Likely Story* (Moon Tide, 2014), and the editor of two anthologies, *The Liberal Media Made Me Do It!* (Nine Toes, 2014) and an ekphrastic e-anthology, *Over the Moon: Birds, Beasts, and Trees—Celebrating the Photography of Beth Moon,* accessible at http://www.poemeleon.org/over-the-moon-birds-beasts-and

Her poems, reviews, articles, and essays have been widely published in journals, anthologies, websites, and web blogs.